Salad is the double agent of the food world. A small portion works as a light, refreshing starter or side while large amounts of leafiness, with tasty add-ins, constitute a complete meal...

now you're cookin'
SALADS

– THIS BOOK JUST MAKES YOU WANNA COOK –

REBO
PUBLISHERS

© 2003 Rebo International b.v. Lisse, The Netherlands

This edition printed in 2010.

Original recipes, photographs, and design: © R&R Publications
Marketing Pty. Ltd., Victoria, Australia

Cover design: Minkowsky Graphics, Enkhuizen, The Netherlands
Typesetting: Artedit Typographic Studio, Prague, Czech Republic
Proofreading: Erin Ferretti Slattery, Elizabeth Haas

ISBN 978 90 366 1979 0

now you're cookin'
SALADS

Foreword

Salads are delicious and versatile: keep them small for a tasty appetizer or meatless side dish, or add all sorts of extras to turn them into a main meal. Drawing inspiration from the farmers' market, produce aisle of the supermarket, or even from your own garden, you'll find recipes in this book for creating the perfect salad.

With inspired and easy-to-prepare salads like Roasted Beet Salad with Balsamic and Dill and Gingered Almond and Broccoli Salad with Cellophane Noodles, these recipes take advantage of each season's freshest and most colorful offerings. Clear recipes and stunning photography help you envision and quickly prepare these healthful, flavorful dishes.

U.S. KITCHEN CONVERSION
(LIQUID OR VOLUME, APPROXIMATE)

1 tsp. = 1/3 tbsp./5 ml
1 tbsp. = 1/2 fl. oz./15 ml
2 tbsp. = 1 fl. oz./30 ml
1/4 cup = 2 fl. oz./60 ml
1/3 cup = 2 2/3 fl. oz./79 ml
1/2 cup = 4 fl. oz./118 ml
2/3 cup = 5 1/3 fl. oz./158 ml
3/4 cup = 6 fl. oz./177 ml
7/8 cup = 7 fl. oz./207 ml
1 cup = 8 fl. oz./237 ml

Avocado, Mango, and Papaya Salad

Serves 4

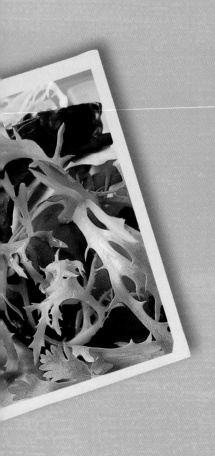

PREPARATION

To make the dressing, peel the mango, slice the flesh off the pit, and chop roughly. Blend to a thin purée with the vinegar, lime juice, oil, ginger, and honey in a food processor. Alternatively, press the mango flesh through a sieve, and mix with the other dressing ingredients.

Halve and peel the avocados, discarding the stones; finely slice the halves lengthwise. Add the lime juice to prevent the avocado from turning brown.

Halve the papayas. Scoop out and discard the seeds. Peel and finely slice the flesh. Arrange on plates, along with the avocado and salad leaves. Pour the dressing over and garnish with the cilantro.

INGREDIENTS

2 ripe avocados
juice of 1/2 lime
2 papayas
1 cup (50 g) mixed lettuce
fresh cilantro, to garnish

DRESSING

1 ripe mango
1 tbsp. rice-wine vinegar or 1 tsp. white-wine
vinegar

juice of 1 lime
1/2 tsp. sesame oil
1/2-inch (1 cm) piece fresh root
ginger, finely chopped
1/2 tsp. honey

Roasted Beet, Orange, and Fennel Salad

Serves 6–8

PREPARATION

Heat the oven to 350°F (180°C).
Wash and trim the beet roots and stems but do not peel the beets.
In a small bowl, mix together the brown sugar, salt, rosemary,
and olive oil until well blended. Toss the whole beets in this
mixture, making sure that the beet skins are all shiny.
Wrap each beet in foil and place in a baking dish.
Roast for approximately 1 hour or until just tender.
Peel the beets and cut them into thick slices.

Very finely slice the fennel bulb and peel the oranges, trimming
any white pith. Cut the orange into segments.

Next, make the dressing. Combine the dill, balsamic vinegar,
olive oil, and salt and pepper to taste and whisk well until thick.
Arrange the beets on a serving platter with the thinly sliced
fennel and orange. Drizzle the dill vinaigrette over the salad,
and scatter the crushed hazelnuts on top.

INGREDIENTS

5 large beets
1 tbsp. brown sugar
1 tsp. salt
2 tbsp. chopped fresh rosemary
3 tbsp. olive oil
1 fennel bulb
3 blood oranges
1 1/3 cups (150 g) toasted hazelnuts,
crushed

DRESSING

1/2 cup (10 g) chopped dill
2 tbsp. balsamic vinegar
1/2 cup (4 fl. oz./120 ml)
olive oil
salt and pepper to taste

Middle-Eastern Bean and Artichoke Salad

Serves 6–8

INGREDIENTS

1 lb, 5 oz. (600 g) green beans

1 3/4 lb. (800 g) canned chickpeas

8 preserved (in brine or oil) artichoke hearts, quartered

1 small red onion, peeled and very finely sliced

1 medium carrot, grated

1/2 cup (10 g) chopped parsley

1/2 cup (10 g) chopped cilantro

2 tbsp. fresh dill

2 tbsp. white-wine vinegar

3 tbsp. olive oil, 1 clove garlic, minced

1 tsp. mustard, 1 tsp. ground cumin

juice of 1 large lemon

salt and pepper to taste

1 cup (100 g) hazelnuts, toasted and roughly chopped

PREPARATION

Steam, boil, or microwave the beans until bright green and crisp-tender. Drain well and refresh in cold water; then cut diagonally in half.

Place the beans in a large bowl and add the drained and rinsed chickpeas, quartered artichoke hearts, finely sliced Spanish onion, grated carrot, parsley, cilantro, and dill.

Stir to combine thoroughly. In a bowl, whisk together the vinegar, olive oil, garlic, mustard, cumin, lemon juice, and salt and pepper. When emulsified, pour over the vegetable mixture and toss very well to coat the vegetables. Sprinkle with toasted hazelnuts and serve.

Marinated Mushrooms on a Bed of Lettuce

Serves 4

INGREDIENTS

3 cups (12 oz./350 g) mixed
mushrooms, such as shiitake,
button, and oyster, sliced thickly
1 cup (3 1/2 oz./100 g) baby
spinach leaves
1/4 cup (1 oz./25 g) watercress,
thick stems discarded
fresh thyme, to garnish

DRESSING
3 tbsp. extra-virgin olive oil

2 tbsp. unsweetened apple juice
2 tsp. tarragon white-wine vinegar
2 tsp. Dijon mustard, 1 clove garlic, crushed
1 tbsp. mixed chopped fresh herbs, such
as oregano, thyme, chives, basil, and parsley
black pepper

PREPARATION

To make the dressing, add the oil, apple juice,
vinegar, mustard, garlic, herbs, and black pepper
to a bowl and whisk together to mix thoroughly.

Pour the dressing over the mushrooms and stir well.
Cover and place in the fridge for 2 hours.

Arrange the spinach and watercress
on serving plates. Spoon the mushrooms
and a little of the dressing over the top
and toss lightly to mix.
Garnish with fresh thyme.

Roasted Beet Salad with Balsamic and Dill

Serves 4–6

PREPARATION

If the beets have their tops attached, remove them and set aside.
Wash the beets and scrub them until clean. Trim the bottom if necessary,
but be careful not to cut too much off the beet.

Toss the beets and olive oil together and place them in a baking dish.
Cover with foil or a lid and roast at 400°F (200°C) for 30–45 minutes
or until tender.

Remove the beets from the oven and cool; peel and discard the skin.
Cut the beets in half lengthwise and add salt and pepper to taste.

Meanwhile, wash the greens thoroughly to remove all traces of sand
and grit. Heat the butter in a sauté pan and add the greens.
Toss for 1 minute until wilted. Remove the greens, add the balsamic
vinegar, and bring to a boil, whisking with the butter. Return the peeled
beets to the pan. Toss them in the balsamic until it has reduced and
leaves a shiny sheen on the beetroots.

Transfer the beets to a platter or bowl and arrange with the wilted beet
greens. Scatter the dill and roasted hazelnuts over, adding spoonfuls
of sour cream or yogurt if desired. Add black pepper to taste.

INGREDIENTS

24 very small beets, preferably with greens attached
1 tbsp. olive oil
salt and freshly ground pepper to taste
1 tbsp. butter
2 tbsp. balsamic vinegar
3 tbsp. fresh dill, snipped
1 cup (100 g) hazelnuts, roasted and chopped
2 tbsp. sour cream or yogurt (optional)
black pepper to taste

Asian-Style Ginger Coleslaw

Serves 6

INGREDIENTS

1/2 large head kale, very finely sliced, about 5 cups (335 g)

4 baby bok choy, leaves separated and sliced

8 green onions, julienned lengthwise

7 oz. (200 g) canned sliced water chestnuts, drained

2 medium carrots, finely julienned

2 stalks lemongrass, very finely sliced, 4 kaffir lime leaves, very finely sliced

DRESSING
2 tbsp. low-fat mayonnaise

2 tbsp. low-fat yogurt, juice of 2 lemons juice of 1 lime, 1 tbsp. freshly grated ginger

4 tbsp. rice vinegar, salt and pepper to taste

GARNISH
1 bunch cilantro, washed well and chopped

1/2 cup (2 1/2 oz./70 g) toasted peanuts or sunflower seeds

PREPARATION

Finely slice the cabbage and mix in a large bowl with the sliced bok choy, julienne spring onions, water chestnuts, julienne carrots and finely sliced lemon grass and lime leaves. Toss thoroughly.

In a bowl, whisk together all the dressing ingredients until smooth and well seasoned. Pour over the salad ingredients and toss thoroughly until all the vegetables are coated with the dressing.

To serve, mix the cilantro in at the last minute and sprinkle with the crushed peanuts or sunflower seeds.

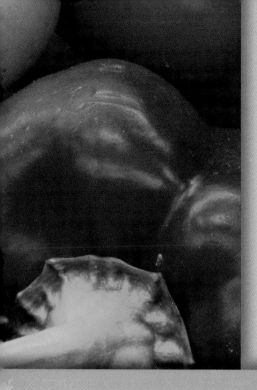

Asian Bok Choy Chicken Salad

Serves 6-8

PREPARATION

If using dried shiitake mushrooms, soak in hot water for 15 minutes before draining and slicing. If using fresh shiitakes, slice finely. Soak the black cloud fungus for 15 minutes; drain. Rinse the soaked mushrooms thoroughly in cold water.

Place the shredded cooked chicken in a large bowl. Break up the cooked noodles under hot running water until the noodles have separated. Shake off excess water and add to the chicken. Add the mushrooms, sliced snow peas, washed baby bok choy leaves, diced bell pepper, sliced spring onions, and water chestnuts. Toss well.

In a bowl, whisk together the ginger, yogurt, kecap manis, hoisin, mirin, rice vinegar, sweet chile sauce, fish sauce, lime juice, and salt and pepper to taste. Add to the chicken salad and toss very well until all the ingredients are coated. Garnish with the toasted slivered almonds and chopped chervil and serve.

INGREDIENTS

8 fresh or dried shiitake mushrooms

1/4 cup (10 g) black cloud fungus

4 cups (800 g) shredded, cooked, skinless chicken

1 kg (2 lb.) fresh Asian Hokkien noodles

2 cups (200 g) fresh snow peas, diagonally sliced

4 baby bok choy, washed well, leaves separated, 1 diced red bell pepper

4 spring onions, finely sliced

canned sliced water chestnuts, drained

1 tbsp. freshly minced ginger

1/4 cup (2 fl. oz./60 ml) plain, low-fat yogurt, 3 tbsp. kecap manis (Indonesian sweet soy sauce)

1 tbsp. hoisin sauce (Chinese barbecue sauce), 3 tbsp. mirin (sweet Japanese rice wine), 3 tbsp. rice vinegar

3 tbsp. sweet chili sauce

1 tbsp. fish sauce, juice of 1 lime

salt and pepper to taste

2 tbsp. slivered almonds, toasted

1 bunch of chervil, parsley, or cilantro

Summer Vegetables with Lime and Cilantro

Serves 4–6

INGREDIENTS

1/2 lb. (250 g) snow peas, ends trimmed
2 bunches of asparagus, stalks halved
1/2 lb. (250 g) sugar snap peas, ends trimmed
1/2 lb. (250 g) fresh peas, shelled, 1/2 lb. (250 g) cherry tomatoes, halved

DRESSING

2 tbsp. lime juice
3 tbsp. chopped cilantro
1/2 cup (4 fl. oz./125 ml) olive oil
1 tbsp. white-wine vinegar

PREPARATION

Blanch the snow peas, asparagus, and sugar snap peas in boiling water for 30 seconds; drain and refresh in a bowl of iced cold water. Drain well.

Blanch the fresh peas in boiling water for 5 minutes, or until tender; drain and refresh in iced water. Drain well. Combine all vegetables and cherry tomatoes.

For the dressing, whisk all ingredients until well combined. Toss over the vegetables and serve.

Summer Salad with Chive Dressing

Serves 4

PREPARATION

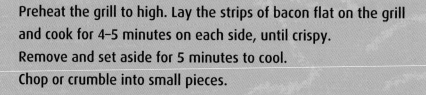

Preheat the grill to high. Lay the strips of bacon flat on the grill
and cook for 4–5 minutes on each side, until crispy.
Remove and set aside for 5 minutes to cool.
Chop or crumble into small pieces.

Put the salad leaves into a large bowl or onto a large platter;
scatter the sliced mushrooms and peppers over the top.
Add the tomato quarters and the Gruyère matchsticks.
Scatter the bacon pieces over and season with salt and pepper.

To make the dressing, put the vinegar, mustard, and oil into
a bowl or screwtop jar and stir or shake well to combine. Stir in
the snipped chives, pour the dressing over the salad, and serve.

INGREDIENTS

1/4 lb. (125 g) smoked bacon
1/4 lb. (125 g) bag mixed lettuce
1 cup (75 g) mushrooms, sliced thinly
1 green or yellow pepper, halved, deseeded
and thinly sliced
4 tomatoes, quartered
1/4 lb. (125 g) Gruyère cheese, cut into
matchstick-sized pieces
salt and black pepper
1 tbsp. wine vinegar, 1 tsp. French mustard
4 tbsp. olive oil, 1 tbsp. snipped fresh chives

Gingered Almond and Broccoli Salad with Noodles

Serves 6–8

INGREDIENTS

3 1/2 oz. (100 g) dried cellophane noodles, 2 tbsp. fish sauce
2 tbsp. rice vinegar
2 tbsp. mirin (sweet Japanese rice wine), 1 tsp. brown sugar
1/2 cup (10 g) chopped fresh cilantro

SALAD

1 tbsp. peanut oil
1 tbsp. grated fresh ginger
1 very finely sliced small red chili pepper, 4 cloves garlic, minced,
4 green onions, minced
1 lb. (500 g) broccoli florets, trimmed
10 fresh shiitake mushrooms, sliced
7 oz. (200 g) baby corn, 3 tbsp. soy sauce,
3 tbsp. mirin, extra, 2 tbsp. rice vinegar,
1 head romaine lettuce, shredded, 1 scant cup
(120 g) blanched almonds, toasted,
extra cilantro, to garnish

PREPARATION

First, prepare the noodles. Fill a deep bowl with very warm water and soak the cellophane noodles for about 10 minutes or until they are soft and tender. Drain. Mix together the fish sauce, rice vinegar, 2 tablespoons of mirin, and the sugar. Toss with the cellophane noodles. Add the cilantro, mix well, and set aside.

Heat the peanut oil in a wok and add the ginger, chopped chile, garlic, and spring onions. Toss thoroughly until the spring onions have wilted, about 3 minutes.

Add the broccoli florets and toss well until bright green. Add the mushrooms and corn and continue tossing over high heat. Add the soy sauce, 3 tablespoons of mirin, and rice vinegar. Continue cooking for 1 minute.

Add the noodles and mix well; remove the pan from the heat.

Divide the shredded lettuce among the plates and top with the broccoli-noodle mixture. Garnish with toasted almonds and fresh chopped cilantro.

Spinach Salad

Serves 4

PREPARATION

Wash and dry the spinach. Remove the fibrous stems and center leaf veins. Slice the onion and eggs into rings. Mix all the ingredients together and toss with the dressing.

To make the dressing, in a blender, combine the sour cream and onion until smooth. Let stand in the refrigerator for at least 2 hours. Add the vinegar and season with salt and pepper.

INGREDIENTS

1 lb. (500 g) young spinach
1 large red onion, 3 hard-boiled eggs
1 generous cup (155 g) black olives

DRESSING

1/4 cup (2 fl. oz./60 ml) sour cream
1 medium-size onion, chopped
1 tbsp. red-wine vinegar
salt and pepper

Tuscan Panzanella with Roasted-Tomato Vinaigrette

Serves 8–10

PREPARATION

Cut the bread into cubes and toss with 2 tablespoons olive oil and the rosemary. Spread out on a baking tray and bake at 400°F (200°C) for 5 minutes until golden; cool.

To make the dressing, heat a heavy pan and brush the tomatoes with a little olive oil. Cook these whole tomatoes in the pan until well blackened all over. Purée with the remaining olive oil, vinegars, garlic, and salt and pepper to taste. Set aside.

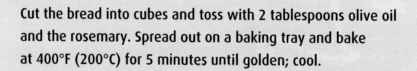

Remove the seeds from the other tomatoes and chop into small chunks. Peel the cucumber and remove the seeds by running a teaspoon along the core. Slice finely. Finely chop the red onion. Pit the olives.

In a bowl, place the toasted bread cubes, tomatoes, cucumber, Spanish onion, olives and torn basil leaves. Add the chopped mint and marjoram. Mix well. Pour the dressing over and toss thoroughly. Allow to sit for 10 minutes; then serve.

INGREDIENTS

1/2 loaf stale, rustic Italian-style bread,
2 tbsp. olive oil
2 tbsp. fresh rosemary, chopped
2 lb. (1 kg) assorted tomatoes
1 cucumber
1 small red onion
20 kalamata olives
20 basil leaves
4 mint leaves, finely sliced
1 tbsp. fresh marjoram

DRESSING

4 small tomatoes
1/2 cup (4 fl. oz./120 ml)
good-quality olive oil
2 tbsp. red-wine vinegar
1 tbsp. balsamic vinegar
3 cloves garlic
salt and freshly ground pepper

Calabrian Salad

Serves 6

PREPARATION

Cover the potatoes in cold water and boil until just tender
all the way through, about 15–20 min.

Drain and leave aside until just cool enough to handle,
then peel and slice thinly.

Cut the tomatoes in half and remove the hard inner core.
Slice the tomatoes and add them to the potatoes.
Add the finely sliced red onions and toss well.

Add the basil, oregano, olive oil, vinegar, and add a little salt
and pepper. Toss everything carefully and serve immediately.

INGREDIENTS

4 large potatoes, scrubbed and washed,
not peeled
8 firm Roma tomatoes
3 red onions, peeled and sliced thinly,
soaked in cold water for 30 minutes
15 small, whole basil leaves
1 heaped tsp. dried oregano
4 tbsp. olive oil
3 tbsp. white-wine or red-wine vinegar
salt and pepper, to taste

NOTE

Salads like this one are perfect
summer accompaniments
to meat, chicken, or fish dishes
but also make wonderful
entrées. This dish is full
of robust flavors and is lovely
as part of an antipasto platter.

31

Warm Vegetable Salad with Serrano Ham

Serves 4

INGREDIENTS

salt and black pepper
2 leeks, white parts only, sliced
1 cup (200 g) shelled broad beans
or garden peas
3/4 cup (150 g)
sugar snap peas
3 tbsp. olive oil
1 clove garlic, thinly sliced
3 spring onions, cut into 2-inch
(5 cm) lengths

1 cup (75 g) baby spinach
3 slices Serrano ham, cut into thin slices
2 large Portobello mushrooms,
very thinly sliced
a few drops of lemon juice
Parmesan shavings, to serve (optional)

PREPARATION

Bring a large saucepan of lightly salted water to the boil. Add the leeks, broad beans or peas and cook for 2 minutes. Add the sugar snap peas and stir for a few seconds. Drain and set aside.

Add 2 tablespoons of oil to the pan, and then add the garlic and spring onions. Stir for a minute to soften slightly; tip in the spinach and stir until it starts to wilt. Add the cooked vegetables to the pan with the remaining oil. Lightly season and fry for 2 minutes, to heat through.

Add the ham to the pan and heat through for 1–2 minutes. Arrange the mixture on a serving plate. Scatter the mushrooms over and sprinkle with lemon juice. Scatter the Parmesan over, if using, and season with black pepper.

Watercress and Pear Salad

Serves 6–8

PREPARATION

Wash and dry the watercress well.

Whisk the olive oil, lemon juice, and white-wine vinegar with salt and pepper until the mixture has thickened slightly.

Slice pears finely and combine with watercress in a bowl.

Drizzle just enough dressing over to coat the leaves. Place on a platter and top with shavings of Parmesan.

INGREDIENTS

2 bunches of watercress,
picked and washed
3 tbsp. olive oil
1 tbsp. lemon juice
1/2 tbsp. white-wine vinegar
salt and pepper
3 Bosc pears, finely sliced
shavings of Parmesan

Carrot and Pecan Salad

Serves 6

PREPARATION

Combine the shredded carrots, raisins, and pecans in a bowl.

Moisten with dressing made by shaking the ingredients
together in a screw-top jar.

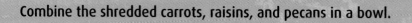

Arrange on washed and crisp lettuce leaves
on individual plates or on one serving dish.

INGREDIENTS

1/2 lb. (250 g) carrots, shredded
1/3 cup (90 g) raisins
6–8 pecan halves, chopped
1 head romaine lettuce

DRESSING

2 tbsp. olive oil
2 tsp. hazelnut or walnut oil
(optional)
1 tbsp. lemon juice
salt and pepper

Marinated Chicken Salad with Warm Dressing

Serves 4

INGREDIENTS

4 boneless, skinless chicken breasts, cut into 1/2-inch (1 cm) strips

2 tbsp. peanut oil

2 tbsp. sesame oil

2 cloves garlic, chopped

1–2 red or green chilis, deseeded and finely sliced

1-inch (2 1/2 cm) piece fresh root ginger, finely grated

1/3 cup (3 fl. oz./75 ml) red wine vinegar

1/3 lb. (160 g) lettuce and mixed fresh herbs

MARINADE

2 tbsp. dark soy sauce

2 tbsp. clear honey

1 tbsp. sesame oil (optional)

PREPARATION

To make the marinade, mix together the soy sauce, honey, and sesame oil, if using. Place the chicken in a non-metallic bowl and cover with the marinade. Toss the chicken well to coat. Cover and refrigerate for 30 minutes.

Heat 1 tablespoon of the peanut oil and 1 tablespoon of the sesame oil in a wok or large, heavy-based frying pan. Add the chicken and stir-fry for 5–6 minutes, until cooked through and browned. Remove from the pan and leave to cool.

Add the remaining oil, garlic, chilis, and ginger to the pan. Fry, while stirring and scraping the bottom of the pan, for 3–4 minutes until the garlic starts to brown. Stir in the vinegar and ⅓ cup (2 ½ fl. oz./75 ml) of water, bring to a boil, and remove from the heat.

Arrange the lettuce on plates, top with the chicken strips, and spoon the warm dressing over.

Chicken and Orange Salad

PREPARATION

Using a small, sharp knife, peel the oranges, working over
a small bowl to reserve the juice. Cut the flesh into segments
and place in a separate bowl.

Stir in the cooked, shredded chicken, celery, green onions
and yellow pepper, and season well. Meanwhile,
make the dressing: mix all the ingredients together, including
the reserved orange juice, in a small bowl until well combined.

Arrange the mixed lettuce and chicken mixture among
four plates and drizzle with dressing.

INGREDIENTS

2 oranges
2 chicken breast filets, cooked and
shredded
2 celery stalks, cut into fine strips
2 green onions, finely shredded
1 yellow bell pepper, deseeded and cut
into fine strips
sea salt and freshly ground black pepper
1/2 lb. (250 g) mixed lettuce

DRESSING

2/3 cup (5 fl. oz./150 ml)
natural yogurt,
2 tbsp. mayonnaise
2 tsp. honey
1 tbsp. roughly chopped fresh
parsley

Chef's Autumn Salad

PREPARATION

Bring a large saucepan of salted water to the boil.
Add the broccoli, return to the boil, then cook for 1–2 minutes,
until slightly softened. Drain and leave to cool for 15 minutes.
Meanwhile, make the dressing. Mix together the mustard,
lime juice, yogurt, oil, cilantro, and seasoning.

Place the lettuce, red onion, cucumber, broccoli, celery,
carrots, and apples in a large bowl. Pour the dressing over
and toss to coat. Arrange the turkey or ham slices in the center
of a shallow serving dish or platter and spoon the salad around
the edge. Scatter the raisins and peanuts over, if using.

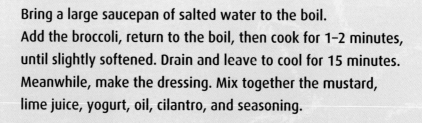

INGREDIENTS

salt and black pepper
1 1/4 cups (225 g) broccoli,
cut into small florets
1 head romaine lettuce, leaves torn
1 red onion, halved and sliced
1/2 cucumber, peeled and sliced
2 stalks celery, sliced
2 carrots, cut into matchstick-sized pieces
2 apples, sliced
7 oz. (200 g) wafer-thin cooked turkey
or ham slices, 2 tbsp. raisins

2 tbsp. roasted salted peanuts,
chopped (optional)

DRESSING

1 tsp. Dijon mustard
juice of 1/2 lime
2/3 cup (5 fl. oz./150 g)
low-fat natural yogurt
2 tbsp. olive oil
1 tbsp. chopped fresh cilantro

Warm Chicken-Liver Salad

Serves 4

INGREDIENTS

4 cups (200 g) mixed lettuce
1 lb. (500 g) frozen chicken livers, defrosted
1 tbsp. olive oil, 1 tbsp. butter
2 tbsp. chopped mixed fresh herbs, such as flat-leaf parsley, sage, marjoram, or thyme
2 cloves garlic, crushed
salt and black pepper

DRESSING

6 tbsp. olive oil
1 tbsp. wine vinegar
juice of 1/2 lemon
2 tsp. Dijon mustard
2 tsp. clear honey

PREPARATION

Place the salad leaves in a large bowl.
To make the dressing, mix the oil, vinegar, lemon juice, mustard, and honey together, and set aside.

Cut the chicken livers into large pieces, removing any fibrous parts. Heat the oil and butter in a large heavy-based frying pan. Add the livers, fresh herbs, garlic, and seasoning. Cook over medium to high heat for 5–8 minutes, until browned on all sides. Remove the livers and place on top of the salad.

Pour the dressing into the pan, stir vigorously to mix with the pan juices and cook for 3 minutes, or until reduced slightly. Pour the dressing over the salad, toss well, and serve.

Warm Salad of Mustard-Glazed Chicken with Red-Wine Vinaigrette

Serves 8

PREPARATION

Make the marinade. Grind 2 tablespoons of the mustard seeds into powder. Mix the ground seeds with the malt vinegar, honey, molasses, brown sugar, olive oil, Dijon mustard, garlic, and boiling water. Whisk well until the mixture is thick and smooth.

Reserve 4 tablespoons of marinade for later use. Place the chicken in a flat glass dish and pour the remaining marinade over. Turn the chicken so that both sides are covered with marinade. Chill for a minimum of 4 hours.

Remove the chicken from the marinade, making sure that each piece has a good coating. Place in an ovenproof baking dish or on a baking sheet and bake at 410°F (210°C) for 20–25 minutes, until cooked through.

Meanwhile, transfer the reserved marinade to a saucepan and bring to a boil. Simmer for 5 minutes; remove from heat. Remove the chicken from the oven and keep warm.

Make a dressing with the red or white wine vinegar and olive oil (with salt and pepper to taste) and a little of the reserved warm marinade. Whisk well. Toss some dressing with the mixed lettuce and spinach leaves just to coat them. Add the spring onions and chopped chives and toss again.

To serve, arrange the salad leaves on plates. Top each plate of salad with a chicken breast sliced on the diagonal. Drizzle remaining warm marinade around the edges of the plate and serve.

INGREDIENTS

FOR SALAD
8 boneless, skinless chicken-breast filets
1 cup (300 g) assorted baby lettuce leaves, washed well and dried
1 cup (300 g) baby spinach leaves, washed well and dried
1 bunch green onions sliced on the diagonal
1 bunch chives, chopped

FOR MARINADE
3 tbsp. mustard seeds

3 tbsp. malt vinegar
2 tbsp. honey
1 tbsp. molasses
1 tbsp. brown sugar
1/2 cup (4 fl. oz./120 ml) olive oil
4 tbsp. Dijon mustard
2 cloves garlic, minced
1/2 cup (4 fl. oz./120 ml) boiling water

FOR DRESSING
2 tbsp. red or white wine vinegar
2 tbsp. olive oil
salt and pepper to taste

Sautéed Duck Salad with Thyme and Honey

Serves 4

PREPARATION

Heat the oven to 370°F (190°C). Season duck breast with
a little salt and pepper.

Heat peanut oil in a pan until almost smoking. Add the duck breast,
skin side down, and cook on high heat until the skin is a deep caramel
brown. Transfer the pan containing the duck to the preheated
oven until the duck is cooked rare, 7–10 minutes.
(Do not turn the duck breasts over.)

Remove the pan from the oven and remove the breasts from the pan,
keeping them warm. Drain and discard the excess fat. Add the butter.
When it begins to bubble, add the thyme leaves and honey.
When simmering, replace duck breasts, skin side up.

Cook for a further minute on low heat, and then remove pan from heat.

Whisk together the lemon juice, walnut oil, salt, pepper, and the pan
juices and mix well. Toss the lettuce leaves and pomegranate with
a little of the dressing.

Divide the lettuce leaves between the plates; garnish with tomatoes.
Slice duck breast and arrange around the salad, drizzling any excess
honey sauce over the duck slices. Garnish with basil leaves and serve.

INGREDIENTS

3 duck breasts, skin on
salt and pepper
1 tbsp. peanut oil
2 tsp. butter
1 sprig thyme, leaves picked from the stalk
2 tbsp. honey
1 tbsp. lemon juice
2 tbsp. walnut oil
fine gray sea salt and cracked black pepper
2 cups (200 g) mixed baby lettuce leaves,

washed and spun dry
1 pomegranate (optional), seeds and pulp scooped out
6 large cherry tomatoes
basil leaves, to garnish

Summer Salad of Grilled Chicken and Mango

Serves 6

PREPARATION

Slice the tomatoes in half lengthwise, and top with sliced basil, mint, salt, pepper, and sugar. Bake at 320°F (160°C) for 2 hours. In a large jug, whisk together all the dressing ingredients until emulsified.

Marinate the chicken in ½ cup (4 fl. oz./120 ml) of dressing, reserving the remainder for later. Allow the chicken to marinate for 1 hour minimum, or up to 4 hours. Heat a non-stick broiling pan and cook the chicken filets over high heat until cooked through, 2–3 minutes on each side. Transfer the cooked filets to a plate and keep warm.

Steam, microwave, or boil the asparagus until tender; refresh under cold water.
Halve the avocado, and peel and dice the flesh. Slice the green onions diagonally and thinly slice the mushrooms. Dice the mango flesh.

To make the salad, place the well-washed spinach leaves in a large bowl and add the blanched asparagus, sliced spring onions, mushrooms and roasted tomatoes, cut into quarters.
Add the reserved dressing and toss thoroughly.
Divide the salad evenly amongst individual plates and add some mango and avocado cubes. Top with 2 filets of chicken, and a generous sprinkling of the chopped nuts. Serve immediately.

INGREDIENTS

6 plum tomatoes
10 basil leaves
10 mint leaves
salt and pepper
1/2 tsp. sugar
12 small chicken-breast filets
1 bunch of asparagus
1 bunch of green onions
8 firm button mushrooms
3 large handfuls of baby spinach leaves

DRESSING

2 tsp. honey
2 tbsp. balsamic vinegar
3 tbsp. raspberry vinegar
2 tbsp. soy sauce
2 tsp. Dijon mustard
2 tsp. minced ginger
2 cloves garlic, minced
1 tsp. sambal oelek (chili paste)
2 tbsp. lemon juice
2 tbsp. olive oil (optional)
salt and freshly ground pepper

GARNISH

1 avocado, 1/2 cup (50 g)
toasted hazelnuts, lightly
crushed, 1/2 cup (50 g)
toasted brazil nuts, lightly
crushed, 1/2 cup (50 g)
toasted pistachios,
lightly crushed

Anchovy, Egg, and Parmesan Salad

Serves 4

INGREDIENTS

3 medium eggs
2 heads chicory
2 heads romaine or hearts
of romaine, leaves torn
12 anchovy filets in oil, drained
and cut in half lengthwise
1 tbsp. capers, drained
3 cherry tomatoes, halved
1/4 cup (50 g) Parmesan
shavings

3 tbsp. extra-virgin olive oil
juice of 1/2 lemon
salt and black pepper
fresh flat-leaf parsley, to garnish

PREPARATION

Bring a small saucepan of water to a boil. Add the eggs and boil for 10 minutes. Remove from the pan, cool under cold running water, and shell. Cut each egg lengthwise into quarters.

On each serving plate, arrange 8 alternating chicory and lettuce leaves, tips facing outwards, in a star shape. Place 2 egg quarters on the base of 2 opposite lettuce leaves; place 2 anchovy halves on the other 2 opposite lettuce leaves. Scatter the capers over the leaves.

Put a cherry tomato half in the center of each plate and drape 2 anchovy halves over the top. Scatter the Parmesan over the salad, and drizzle with olive oil and lemon juice. Season to taste and garnish with parsley.

Shrimp and Grapefruit Cocktail

Serves 4

PREPARATION

Finely grate 1 teaspoon of grapefruit zest and reserve
for the dressing. Slice the top and bottom off each grapefruit
and cut off the peel and pith, following the curve of the fruit.
Cut between the membranes to release the segments. Reserve.

To make the dressing, place the mayonnaise in a bowl,
and stir in the vinegar, ketchup, Tabasco (if using),
and Worcestershire sauce to taste. Stir in the grapefruit zest,
tarragon, and sour cream. Season.

Arrange the lettuce in serving bowls. Set aside.

Reserve some shrimp in the shell for garnish, and shell
the remainder. Rinse and dry on kitchen towels,
mix with the grapefruit segments, and mound onto the lettuce.
Spoon the dressing over, sprinkle with paprika, and garnish
with the unpeeled shrimp. Serve with lemon wedges.

INGREDIENTS

2 pink or ruby red grapefruit

2 heads romaine or hearts of romaine, shredded

1 lb. (450 g) large, cooked, shell-on shrimp, defrosted if frozen

paprika, for dusting

lemon wedges, to serve

DRESSING

6 tbsp. mayonnaise

1 tbsp. tarragon white-wine vinegar

2 tbsp. ketchup

a few drops Tabasco sauce (optional)

1–2 tsp. Worcestershire sauce

2 tsp. chopped fresh tarragon

2 tbsp. sour cream

salt and black pepper

Crab Salad with Tomato Dressing

Serves 4

PREPARATION

To make the dressing, place the tomatoes in a bowl and cover
with boiling water. Leave for 30 seconds; skin, deseed, and cut
into small dice. Whisk the oil and vinegar together in a bowl;
then whisk in the cream, tarragon, and seasoning.
Add sugar and Worcestershire sauce to taste,
and stir in the tomatoes and cucumber.

Mix together the crabmeat and sliced fennel.
Stir in 4 tablespoons of the dressing. Arrange the salad leaves
together with the crab mixture on plates. Spoon the remaining
dressing over; sprinkle with chives, chopped fennel tops
and paprika or cayenne pepper.

INGREDIENTS

2 large dressed crabs
(about 250 g crabmeat)
1 large bulb fennel, thinly sliced, top
chopped and reserved for garnish
1 1/2 cups (80 g) mixed lettuce
1 tbsp. snipped fresh chives
paprika or cayenne pepper to garnish

DRESSING

2 large tomatoes
5 tbsp. olive oil
1 tbsp. white wine vinegar
4 tbsp. cream
1 tsp. chopped fresh tarragon
salt and black pepper
pinch of superfine sugar
dash of Worcestershire sauce
2-inch (5 cm) piece cucumber,
diced

Fijian Kokoda

PREPARATION

Cut the fish into ½-inch (1 cm) cubes and mix with 1 scant cup (7 fl. oz./200 ml) of the lime juice, half the coconut milk, and salt and pepper to taste. Stir well and marinate overnight or for at least 4 hours.

When the fish is firm and looks opaque (cooked), drain away and discard the liquid.

Mix the drained fish with the bell-pepper pieces, chili, and tomato. Add the remaining coconut milk and lime juice and stir to combine thoroughly.

Serve cold in glasses with wedges of lime or lemon as an entrée.

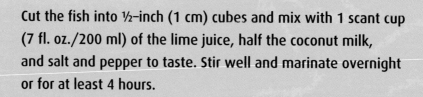

INGREDIENTS

3 1/2 lb. (1 1/2 kg) firm white fish
1 cup fresh lime or lemon juice
1 1/8 cup (10 fl. oz./300 ml) canned coconut milk
salt and pepper to taste
1 small red bell pepper, finely diced
1 small green bell pepper, finely diced
1 small red chili, minced
1 firm tomato, finely diced
lime or lemon wedges, for garnish

Spanish
Shrimp Salad

Serves 4–6

INGREDIENTS

2 cups (370 g) long-grain rice
3 cups (24 fl. oz./710 ml) water
4 tbsp. olive oil
1/2 tsp. saffron threads
soaked in 2 tsp. warm water
1 tbsp. lemon juice
zest of 1/2 lemon
1 cup (150 g) black olives,
pitted salt and pepper

18 oz. (500 g) cooked shrimp
2 tbsp. chopped basil or parsley
3 red bell peppers, cut into strips
lettuce leaves, for serving
3 tomatoes, peeled and diced

PREPARATION

Cook the rice, per package instructions,
with the saffron. Spread out to cool. Put all the salad
ingredients into a bowl and mix well. Combine the dressing
ingredients in a screw-topped jar and shake well.
Pour the dressing over the salad and mix gently.

Serve on a bed of lettuce leaves.
If desired, reserve some of the strips of pepper,
olives, and shrimp to garnish the rice.

Warm Salmon Salad

Serves 4

PREPARATION

Cook the eggs in simmering water for about 7 minutes.
Add the green beans and cook for a further 3 minutes.
Drain and set the green beans aside;
shell and quarter the eggs and set aside.

Meanwhile, wash the fish filets and dry them with paper towels.
Place the filets in a shallow frying pan. Barely cover with water
and bring to a boil. Cover and simmer for 5 minutes. Remove from
heat and leave for 5 minutes, or until cooked and beginning to flake.
Drain the fish, remove the skin, and flake into pieces.

For the dressing, combine all the ingredients together in a small
bowl. Heat 2 inches (5 cm) oil in a frying pan, over high heat, and fry
he potatoes for 5–6 minutes, until golden and crisp. Drain on paper
towels and season with salt. In a large bowl, combine the beans,
eggs, flaked salmon, onion, cherry tomatoes, and dressing.
To serve, arrange the salad leaves on plates, top with the salmon
and potatoes, and garnish with basil leaves.

INGREDIENTS

3 medium eggs
generous 1/2 cup (75 g) green beans,
  chopped
3 salmon filets
sunflower oil, for deep frying
8 oz. (225 g) baby new potatoes
  sliced very thinly
1 small red onion, finely sliced
1 cup (125 g) cherry tomatoes, halved
4 oz. (120 g) mixed lettuce
fresh basil leaves, to garnish

DRESSING

4 tbsp. olive oil
2 tsp. red wine vinegar
2 tsp. balsamic vinegar
1 garlic clove, crushed
sea salt and freshly ground
black pepper

Pork Salad
with Vermicelli
Noodles

Serves 4–5

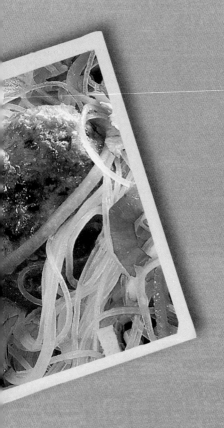

PREPARATION

Combine ground pork, cilantro, fish, chili sauce, and flour.
Mix well.

Shape into small balls and chill for 30 minutes.

Place noodles in a large bowl and cover with boiling water.
Leave until soft, approximately 30 minutes.

Combine dressing ingredients.

Heat oil and cook pork meatballs for 8–10 minutes,
turning to brown, until finished.

Combine noodles, pork meatballs, and carrot.
Pour dressing over and toss well. Serve.

INGREDIENTS

1 lb. (500 g) lean ground pork
3 tbsp. fresh cilantro, finely chopped
2 tsp. fish sauce
2 tbsp. sweet chili sauce
1 tbsp. flour
1 tbsp. oil
10 1/2 oz. (300 g) vermicelli (cellophane) noodles
1 large carrot, cut into thin strips

DRESSING

1 bunch cilantro, finely chopped
1 tbsp. grated ginger
1 red onion, thinly sliced
2 tsp. brown sugar
1/2 cup (4 fl. oz./120 ml) fresh lime juice
2 tbsp. fish sauce
1 1/2 tbsp. peanut oil
1-2 red chilis, finely chopped

Armenian Stuffed Tomato Salad

Serves 8

INGREDIENTS

8 large tomatoes, 4 tbsp. olive oil
1 large onion, chopped finely
1 large leek, green part removed
and finely chopped
3 cups (475 g) steamed
or boiled white or brown rice*
1/2 cup (50 g) toasted
pine nuts
3/4 cup (125 g) golden raisins
1/2 cup (10 g) parsley, chopped
1 tbsp. fresh mint, chopped

3/4 tsp. sea salt
1/2 tsp. black pepper
2 cloves garlic, peeled and crushed
1/2 cup (4 fl. oz./120 ml) vegetable stock
1/2 cup (4 fl. oz./120 ml) white wine
1 lb. (500 g) baby spinach

PREPARATION

With a sharp knife, slice the tops off the tomatoes, and scoop out as much flesh as possible without damaging the exterior of the tomato. Finely chop the tomato pulp.

Heat the olive oil and cook the chopped onion and leek until slightly golden. Add the rice, tomato pulp, nuts, currants, parsley, mint, salt and pepper and sauté until the mixture is hot and well flavored.

Fill each tomato with the rice mixture and replace the tops of the tomatoes. Combine the garlic, stock, and white wine; drizzle around the tomatoes.

Bake at 350°F (180°C) for 15 minutes.

Meanwhile, wash and dry the spinach leaves. When the tomatoes have finished cooking, remove them and toss the remaining hot liquid through the spinach, discarding the garlic.

Serve a mound of warm spinach on each plate with the tomato perched on top. Drizzle any remaining liquid over and serve.

*1 cup uncooked rice = 3 cups cooked rice.

German Potato Salad

Serves 6–8

PREPARATION

Boil the potatoes in their skins until just tender. Drain.
Peel the potatoes while they are still hot and cut them
into slices. Place them in a bowl with the chopped onion.
Bring the stock to a boil with the vinegar;
and while this is boiling, pour it over the potatoes.

Leave to marinate until almost all the liquid is absorbed,
about 20 minutes. Pour off any excess liquid, and gently fold
in the oil and mustard mixed together. Taste, and season
with salt and pepper if necessary. Lastly, fold in the sour cream.
Serve at room temperature, garnished with dill
or other fresh herbs.

INGREDIENTS

6 medium potatoes
1 onion, finely chopped
1 cup (8 fl. oz./250 ml) chicken stock
4 tbsp. white vinegar
5 tbsp. vegetable oil
2 tsp. prepared German mustard
salt and freshly ground white pepper
1/2 cup (4 fl. oz./120 ml) sour cream
dill or other herbs to garnish

Japanese
Rice-Noodle Salad

Serves 4

PREPARATION

Fill a large bowl with warm water and immerse the rice noodles,
allowing them to soak until soft for about 5–10 minutes.
Drain and rinse under cold water to refresh them;
then place the noodles in a large mixing bowl.

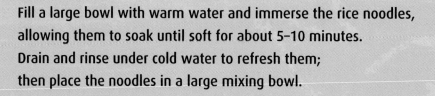

Heat the olive oil in a small non-stick pan and add the ginger
and chilis. Sauté gently for a minute or two.
Add the chopped bell-pepper pieces and raise the heat
to medium high. Stir fry the pieces of pepper until they
are softened. Add the spring onion slices and continue
to cook for a further 2 minutes.

Add the pepper mixture into the mixing bowl with the noodles.
Add the cilantro, tossing thoroughly.

In a small bowl, whisk together the lime juice, rice vinegar,
soy sauce, and stock. Toss with the noodles.
Sprinkle with the sesame seeds and chill before serving.

INGREDIENTS

8 oz. (250 g) long, flat rice noodles
1 tsp. olive oil
2 tsp. freshly grated ginger
1–2 small fresh red chilis, seeded
and minced
1 red bell pepper, cut into small chunks
6 spring onions, sliced diagonally
1/2 bunch cilantro
juice of 1 lime
1 tbsp. Japanese rice vinegar

1 tbsp. soy sauce
2 tbsp. vegetable stock
3 tbsp. sesame seeds

Cabbage and Chinese Noodle Salad

Serves 4-6

INGREDIENTS

SALAD

1/2 head Napa cabbage
4 baby bok choy
8 spring onions
1/2 bunch fresh cilantro
3/4 cup (60 g) flaked almonds, toasted
1/2 cup (68 g) pine nuts, toasted
1 cup (100 g) fried Chinese noodles

DRESSING

4 tbsp. peanut oil
2 tbsp. balsamic vinegar
2 tbsp. fresh lime or lemon juice
1 tbsp. brown sugar (optional)
1 tbsp. soy sauce
salt and ground pepper to taste

PREPARATION

Finely shred the cabbage and transfer to a large mixing bowl. Thoroughly wash the bok choy, slice them across, and add to the cabbage.

Wash the spring onions and slice them finely on the diagonal. Add these to the cabbage mixture together with the washed and roughly chopped cilantro.

Under the griller or in a dry frying pan, toast the almonds and pine nuts and set aside to cool. (Alternatively, toast the nuts in a microwave by spreading the nuts over the microwave plate and cooking them on HIGH for 2 minutes.) Mix gently to distribute then cook for consecutive extra minutes until the nuts are as golden as you wish. Allow to cool.

Mix the nuts and noodles with the cabbage salad.

To make the dressing, whisk all the ingredients together with a whisk until thick. Drizzle over the salad and toss thoroughly then serve immediately.

Smoked Mackerel, Orange, and Lentil Salad

Serves 4

PREPARATION

Cook the lentils in boiling water for 30 minutes
or until tender.

Meanwhile, slice the top and bottom off each orange,
using a small serrated knife and working over a bowl
to catch the juices. Cut away the peel and pith, following
the curve of the fruit. Carefully cut between the membranes
to release the segments. Squeeze the juice from
the membranes into the bowl and reserve for the dressing.
Arrange the watercress, orange segments, and smoked
mackerel in serving bowls.

To make the dressing, mix together the horseradish, oil,
salt, pepper, and the reserved orange juice. Drain the lentils
and stir them into the dressing. Drizzle the dressing over
the salad and serve.

INGREDIENTS

1/4 cup (50 g) lentils
4 small oranges
4 cups (170 g) watercress
14 oz. (400 g) smoked mackerel filet,
skinned and coarsely flaked

DRESSING

4 tbsp. horseradish
4 tbsp. vegetable oil
salt and black pepper

Mexican Tortilla Salad

Serves 4–6

PREPARATION

First, make the dressing. Place all the dressing ingredients
in a blender or food processor and blend until smooth. Set aside.

Next, make the salad. Heat oil in heavy medium saucepan
over medium-high heat.

Add a handful of tortilla strips and cook until crisp,
about 4 minutes per batch. Remove from the oil and drain
on paper towels.

Combine cabbage, lettuce, mango, jicama, onion, bell peppers,
pumpkin seeds, and cilantro in a large bowl. Toss with enough
dressing to coat, adding salt and pepper to taste.
Add the tortilla strips and serve.

INGREDIENTS

oil for frying
4 corn tortillas, cut into strips
3 cups (210 g) thinly shredded green cabbage
3 cups (165 g) thinly shredded iceberg lettuce
1 mango, peeled and flesh diced
1 cup (130 g) diced, peeled jicama
1 red or purple onion, finely diced
3 red bell peppers, roasted, peeled and sliced
1/2 cup (32 g) shelled pumpkin seeds, toasted
1/2 bunch cilantro, chopped
salt and pepper to taste

FOR THE DRESSING

1 small mango, peeled, pitted, diced
1/2 cup (4 fl. oz./120 ml) grapefruit juice
1/4 cup (2 fl. oz./60 ml) fresh lime juice
1–2 small red chilis
4 shallots, chopped
2 tbsp. vegetable oil
1 garlic clove

Spirals with Chicken, Chives, and Thyme

Serves 4 people

PREPARATION

Cook spirals according to the package instructions.
Drain, rinse, and let stand.

Melt the butter in a saucepan.
Add the lemon zest and juice. Stir to combine.

Add the cream, herbs, chicken and pasta.
Toss lightly together until heated through.
Spoon into a bowl, sprinkle with the Parmesan
cheese, and garnish with chives.

Serve as a warm salad with a separate bowl
of mixed lettuce.

INGREDIENTS

3 1/3 cups (350 g) spiral-shaped pasta
2 tbsp. snipped chives
1/4 cup (60 g) butter
1 tbsp. chopped thyme, zest of 1 lemon
3 cups (500 g) cooked chicken, chopped
4 tbsp. lemon juice
1/2 cup (60 g) finely grated Parmesan cheese,
1 1/4 cups (1/2 pint/300 ml) light cream,
chives, to garnish

Tandoori Lamb Salad with Sesame Seeds

Serves 6

PREPARATION

Place the onion, ginger, lemon juice, and water in a food processor with the yogurt, spices, and salt. Process until the mixture is smooth. Remove from the processor and pour over the lamb cutlets, turning to coat both sides of the lamb. Marinate for a minimum of 4 hours or up to 8 hours.

Preheat the oven to 430°F (220°C). When you are ready to cook, mix the sesame seeds and onion seeds together and place them on a plate. Remove the lamb cutlets from the marinade one at a time, allowing the excess marinade to run off. Dip each cutlet in the sesame mixture, coating both sides. Place the coated cutlets on a non-stick baking tray and bake in the preheated oven for 10 minutes for medium rare, or longer if you prefer.

Meanwhile, prepare the salad. Wash and dry the spinach and mixed lettuce leaves and place them, with the green onions, in a large salad bowl. Whisk together the vinegar and oil with salt and pepper to taste; add the few drops of sesame oil, continuing to whisk until the dressing is thick. Toss the salad with the dressing until the leaves are well coated, and divide the salad between 6 plates. Arrange 2 cutlets on each plate and serve immediately.

INGREDIENTS

1 large onion, chopped
1/4 cup (20 g) fresh ginger, grated, juice of
1 lemon, 1 tbsp. water
1/2 cup (4 fl. oz./120 ml) plain yogurt
2 tsp. ground coriander, 2 tsp. ground cumin
1/2 tsp. ground turmeric
1/4 tsp. cayenne, 1 tbsp. garam masala
1/4 tsp. mace, 1 tsp. salt
12 large lamb cutlets,
1 cup (140 g) sesame seeds
1/2 cup (4 g) black onion seeds

4 1/2 cups (250 g) baby
spinach leaves
4 cups (200 g) mixed baby
lettuce leaves
4 green onions, sliced
1/8 cup (1 1/3 fl. oz./40 ml)
white vinegar
1/4 cup (2 fl. oz./60 ml)
peanut oil, a few drops of
toasted sesame oil
salt and pepper to taste

Seared Tuna Salad with Crisp Wontons

Serves 4

PREPARATION

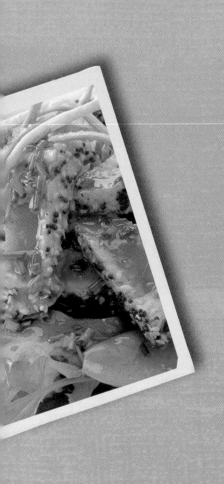

First, make the dressing. Whisk olive oil, lime juice, orange juice, soy sauce, rice vinegar, sesame oil, chives, and ginger in small bowl to blend. Season with salt and pepper.

Heat some oil in a frying pan or wok and add the chile, spring onions, baby corn, and snow peas, tossing over high heat until the vegetables are crisp tender, about 3 minutes. Transfer the hot vegetables to a bowl and drizzle over a little of the dressing. Set aside.

Mix the sesame seeds and black onion seeds on a plate and season the fish with salt and pepper. Press the fish into the seed mixture, coating both sides evenly.

Heat some more oil in the same frying pan used for the vegetables. Add the tuna and sear over high heat until the fish is just cooked through. Transfer to a platter and, when cool, use a sharp knife to slice each filet thinly.

To prepare the wontons, heat some vegetable oil in a wok or frying pan and, when smoking, add the strips of wonton and cook until golden brown. Remove from the pan and drain on paper towels. Add salt to taste.

Toss the lettuce leaves with the cooked vegetable mixture and additional dressing, tossing thoroughly so that the leaves are well coated. Add salt and pepper to taste. Divide the lettuce mixture between 4 plates and top with the sliced seared tuna slices. Arrange a bundle of fried wonton strips on top.

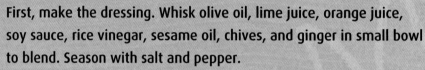

INGREDIENTS

1-2 tbsp. peanut oil, 1 small red chili, minced
8 spring onions, finely sliced on the diagonal
1 cup (100 g) baby corn
1 cup (150 g) snow peas, trimmed
4 tbsp. sesame seeds
4 tbsp. black onion (nigella) seeds
4 tuna steaks, 5 oz. (150 g) each
salt and pepper to taste
vegetable oil (for deep-frying)
8 wonton wrappers, cut into thin strips
4 1/2 cups (250 g) mixed baby lettuce leaves

DRESSING

1/2 cup (4 fl. oz./120 ml) olive oil
1/4 cup (2 fl. oz./60 ml) fresh lime juice, 1/4 cup
(2 fl. oz./60 ml) orange juice,
1/8 cup (1 2/3 fl. oz./50 ml) soy sauce
1/8 cup (1 2/3 fl. oz./50 ml) rice vinegar, 1 tbsp. toasted sesame oil, 1/2 bunch fresh chives, minced, 1 tbsp. fresh ginger, minced salt and pepper to taste

Waldorf Chicken Salad

Serves 4

PREPARATION

Place the chicken in a bowl, and add the celery
and walnuts. Stir to mix. Core and dice the apples.
Toss them with the lemon juice to prevent browning.
Add to the chicken and mix well.

To make the dressing, mix together the mayonnaise,
yogurt, lemon zest, and black pepper in a small bowl.
Add the chicken mixture and toss lightly to mix.
Cover and refrigerate for at least 1 hour before serving.

Arrange the salad leaves on serving plates
and top with the chicken mixture.
Garnish with fresh chives.

INGREDIENTS

1 1/2 cups (175 g) cooked boneless
chicken breasts, skinned and diced
4 sticks celery, thinly sliced
3/4 cup (75 g) walnuts, roughly
chopped, 1 red apple
1 green apple, juice of 1/2 lemon
3 3/4 cups (200 g) mixed lettuce
snipped fresh chives, to garnish

DRESSING

4 tbsp. mayonnaise
4 tbsp. low-fat natural yogurt
1/3 tsp. lemon zest, black pepper

Warm Duck and Mango Salad

Serves 4

INGREDIENTS

1 ripe mango
2 1/2 cups (125 g) mixed dark
lettuce leaves such as baby spinach,
lollo rosso, and arugula
2 1/2 cups (125 g) sugar
snap peas, chopped
4 green onions, sliced diagonally
2 tsp. sesame oil
8 oz. (225 g) boneless duck breast,
skinned and cut into strips
fresh cilantro, to garnish

DRESSING

3 tbsp. extra-virgin olive oil
juice of 1/2 lime, 1 tsp. clear honey
2 tbsp. chopped fresh cilantro
black pepper

PREPARATION

Slice off the 2 fat sides of the mango close to the pit. Cut a criss-crossing pattern across the flesh (but not the skin) of each side with a sharp knife. Push the skin inside out to expose the flesh and cut the cubes off. Place in a salad bowl with the lettuce, sugar snap peas, and green onions. Toss together gently to mix.

To make the dressing, whisk together the olive oil, lime juice, honey, cilantro, and black pepper in a small bowl until thoroughly mixed.

Heat the sesame oil in a wok or large frying pan, add the duck, and stir-fry over a high heat for 4–5 minutes until tender. Add the warm duck to the mango salad, drizzle with dressing, and toss together to mix. Garnish with fresh cilantro.

Warm Lima Bean and Prosciutto Salad with Arugula

Serves 4

PREPARATION

Place the lima beans in a large bowl of warm water
and soak overnight.

The next day, drain the beans and place them in a saucepan
of cold water. Bring to a boil and simmer for 1 hour or until just
tender. Drain, reserving a ladle or two of the cooking water.

Heat the olive oil in a medium saucepan. Add the red-pepper
flakes and garlic, and sauté briefly until the garlic is golden.

Add the prosciutto and stir over moderate heat until beginning
to brown, about 2 minutes. Add the lima beans and cook,
tossing occasionally, until heated through, about 3 minutes,
adding some of the reserved cooking water if the mixture seems
a little dry.

Season with salt and pepper and add the torn basil leaves
and rocket. Toss gently, and serve warm.

INGREDIENTS

1 lb. (500 g) dried lima beans
2 tbsp. olive oil
1/2 tsp. dried red-pepper flakes
3 garlic cloves, minced
1 cup (100 g) prosciutto, roughly chopped
salt and freshly ground pepper
10 basil leaves, torn
2 handfuls of arugula

Warm Mediterranean Pasta Salad

Serves 4

INGREDIENTS

1 3/4 cup (175 g) dried pasta shells
2/3 cup (150 g) green beans, halved
4 green onions, sliced
1 green pepper, deseeded and chopped
1/2 cup (125 g) cherry tomatoes, halved
1 large ripe avocado, halved, stoned and peeled, black pepper
torn fresh basil leaves, to garnish

DRESSING

3 tbsp. olive or sunflower oil
1 tbsp. white wine vinegar
1 tbsp. clear honey, 1 tsp. Dijon mustard

PREPARATION

To make the dressing, place the oil, vinegar, honey and mustard in an empty screw-top jar and shake well to combine.

Cook the pasta shells according to the package instructions. When they are almost cooked, add the green beans and cook for 2 minutes, or until the pasta is tender but still firm to the bite and the beans have softened. Drain well.

Place the pasta and beans in a large bowl with the green onions, green pepper, cherry tomatoes, avocado, and seasoning. Add the dressing and toss well. Garnish with the basil.

Warm Bell-Pepper and Rosemary Salad

Serves 6

PREPARATION

Slice the 4 sides off each bell pepper
and discard the seed core.
Slice the peppers into long, thin strips.

Heat the olive oil in a frying pan.
Add the red onion and rosemary,
and sauté on high heat for 3 minutes.
Add the garlic and all the pepper
pieces and toss thoroughly
with the rosemary-flavored oil.

Continue cooking over low heat
for 30 minutes, stirring often, until
the pepper pieces are wilted and the onion
has caramelized a little. Add the balsamic
vinegar and cook for a further 5 minutes.
Add salt and pepper to taste,
and serve warm.

INGREDIENTS

6 large bell peppers of assorted
colors
2 tbsp. olive oil
1 large red onion, peeled and cut into
eighths
3 tbsp. fresh rosemary
3 cloves garlic, minced
1 tbsp. balsamic vinegar
salt and freshly ground pepper to taste

Warm Tomato Gratin Salad

Serves 6–8

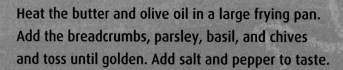

PREPARATION

Heat the butter and olive oil in a large frying pan.
Add the breadcrumbs, parsley, basil, and chives
and toss until golden. Add salt and pepper to taste.

Place the tomatoes on a non-stick baking sheet,
adding salt and pepper to taste. Press the crumb
mixture over the tomatoes to cover each slice.

Bake the tomatoes at 350°F (180°C) for 10 minutes
and then broil, to toast the crumbs.

Meanwhile, toss the lettuce leaves with the combined olive oil
and vinegar, and add salt and pepper to taste.

Arrange the lettuce leaves on a platter and top with the tomato
slices, allowing each to overlap the previous one.
Grind freshly black pepper over and serve.

INGREDIENTS

2 tbsp. melted butter
2 tbsp. olive oil
2 cups (250 g) fresh breadcrumbs
1/2 cup (10 g) chopped parsley
20 large basil leaves, finely sliced
1/2 bunch chives, chopped
salt and cracked black pepper to taste
6–8 large tomatoes, sliced thickly
4 cups (200 g) assorted mixed lettuce leaves

DRESSING

2 tbsp. olive oil
1 tbsp. balsamic vinegar
salt and pepper to taste

Index